UBU TRUMP

or

How 19th-century French literature predicted Donald Trump's retro-autocratic futurism

A tragi-comic play by Rainer Ganahl, after Alfred Jarry

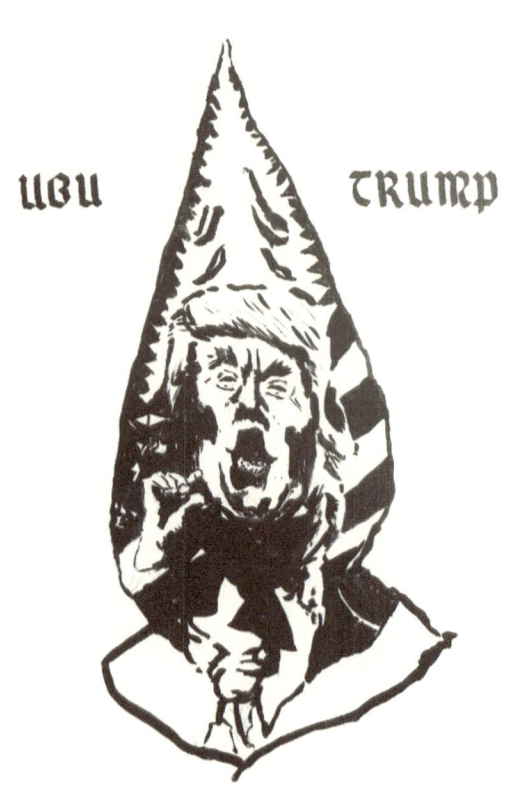

UBU TRUMP

Alfred Jarry first presented his absurdist, expletive-filled play King Ubu in Paris in 1896, and instantly ignited a literary scandal. King Ubu not only influenced artistic movements such as Dada, Surrealism, and the Absurd Theater of Jean Genet and Samuel Beckett, but it anticipated, with frightening perspicacity, the catastrophic political madness of the 21st century. Written in a rudimentary and comically nonsensical way—it even incorporates some of Jarry's high-school stunts—the play lends itself to updating with contemporary slang and subjects. About 10 years ago, Rainer Ganahl rewrote Jarry's text as Ubu Lenin, with Vladimir Lenin and his wife Nadezhda Krupskaya as the protagonists. Now, the advent of Donald Trump has presented an even more appropriately divisive, madcap, narcissistic stand-in for King Ubu. Ganahl's Ubu Trump will take place in Harlem, a neighborhood filled with many of the very people Trump supporters would like to see deported, banned, or put behind "big, beautiful walls." Just like Jarry's King Ubu, Trump and his cronies run their administration like a mafia family business, with barely fig-leafed personal enrichment schemes layered upon corrupt policies and, in all likelihood, treason. In Ubu Trump, the father, King Ubu, has been replaced with Ubu Trump, while Mama Ubu is reincarnated as UBU IVANKA — Originally set in Poland and Russia, the new play blends Warsaw with Washington, and Poland with the USA, alluding to Trump's special dealings with Putin and the new right-wing government in Poland. The actors perform behind three simple graphic panels based on Jarry's own sketches of King Ubu, and overlapped with renderings of the ruling Trump family: Donald, Ivanka, Jared, and their Russian guest, Putin. This theatrical performance will be staged at a morgue in Harlem, the neighborhood where Ganahl has been living for more than 20 years.

UBU TRUMP

by Alfred Jarry updated by Rainer Ganahl, 2017

ACT I, SCENE I

Trump tower

UBU TRUMP — Shit!

UBU IVANKA — Oh! Such language! Papa Ubu Trump, what a pig you are!

UBU TRUMP — Watch out, I'll kill you!

UBU IVANKA — It's not me, you ought to kill, it's someone else.

UBU TRUMP — By my green dick, I don't understand.

UBU IVANKA — What! Papa Ubu, you're content with your lot?

UBU TRUMP — By my green dick. I'm content. After all, I'm Councilor to King Wenceslas, a Knight of the Red Eagle of Poland, and a close advisor to the US President. I am also in possession of the Trump Towers, Golf courses, casinos, Trump University and a flourishing suit business. In addition, I'm hosting the Apprentice and stage all major beauty contests, where ugly women like you don't belong! What more do you want?

UBU IVANKA — Shut up! After being King of Aragon, you're content with parading around fifty losers armed with only cabbage-cutters, when you could put the crown of Poland on your head? And what about the American presidency after Obama had humiliated you at his Correspondence Gala? Don't you think grabbing pussies at the White House is sexier, you dirty old shit?

UBU TRUMP — I don't understand a word you're saying.

UBU IVANKA — You are so stupid.

UBU TRUMP — By my green dick, the King is very much alive. Hasn't he got legions of children?

UBU IVANKA — What prevents you from slaughtering the whole family and putting yourself in their place?

UBU TRUMP — Ubu Ivanka, you do me wrong. Watch out so that you don't end up in the soup.

UBU IVANKA — If I were in your place, I'd want to plant that ass on a throne and, as your supremacist supporters suggest, in the White House. You could make lots of money, fly Air Force One and shit on the world.

UBU TRUMP — If I were King, I'd build a big beautiful wall with Mexico, ban all Muslims and offer a fabulous Big Mac to the Chinese President at Mc Donalds.

UBU IVANKA — The world media would report exclusively about you the way Fox News has been doing it since you declared Obama a Kenyan.

UBU TRUMP — Ah! I yield to temptation.

UBU IVANKA — Papa Trump, now you're acting like a real man.

UBU TRUMP — No, no! Me, slaughtering the King of Poland, the president of the United States, NO - I'd sooner die!

UBU IVANKA *(aside)* — Oh, shit! – (Aloud.) Would you rather remain poor as a rat, Papa Ubu Trump?

UBU TRUMP — By my green dick, I'd rather beg like the hungry and the poor.

UBU IVANKA — And your walls, your news reports, your tax code, and you supreme court justices?

UBU TRUMP — And then what, Ubu Ivanka?

(He leaves)

UBU IVANKA — Fucking shit! He's slow to understand, but he's shaken. Thanks to God in eight days I may be the Queen of Poland and the First Lady of the United States.

Scene II

At Trump tower

UBU IVANKA — Good morning, gentlemen. We've been waiting for you impatiently. Sit down.

MICHAEL FLYNN — Good morning, Madam. Where is Ubu Trump?

UBU TRUMP — Here I am! By my green dick, I'm certainly fat enough to be noticed.

MICHAEL FLYNN — Hello, UBU TRUMP.

UBU TRUMP — Oof! A few more pounds and I'll break the chair.

MICHAEL FLYNN — Well, Madam Ubu Ivanka, what are you serving today?

UBU IVANKA — Polish soup, wombat cutlets, veal, Trump steaks, pate of dog, turkey rumps, dog paste Trump style, charlotte russe...

UBU TRUMP — I guess that's enough. Don't tell me there is more?

UBU IVANKA — Sherbet, salad, fruits, dessert, boiled beef, Jerusalem artichokes, cauliflower a la shit.

UBU TRUMP — Hey! That costs money.

UBU IVANKA — Don't listen to him, Ubu Trump is a cheap imbecile.

UBU TRUMP — To the door, everybody! Michael Flynn, I have to speak to you.

THE OTHERS — Hey! We haven't eaten.

UBU TRUMP — How have you not eaten? To the door, everybody except Flynn.

Nobody leaves

UBU TRUMP — By my green dick, leave, I'm going to murder you with these wombat cutlets.

Scene III

Trump tower

UBU TRUMP — Michael Flynn, I've decided to make you my National Security Advisor.

MICHAEL FLYNN — But how? I thought you were terribly out of favour in Washington, Ubu Trump.

UBU TRUMP — In a few days, if you please, I shall reign over the USA and the Kingdom of Poland.

MICHAEL FLYNN — Are you going to kill King Wenceslas?

UBU TRUMP — He's not silly this guy.

MICHAEL FLYNN — If it's a question of killing the King, I'm in. We have Czar Putin and WikiLeaks on our side.

UBU TRUMP — Oh! oh! I love you, Michael.

MICHAEL FLYNN — Hey! You stink, Ubu Trumpo Don't you ever wash?

UBU TRUMP — Rarely.

UBU IVANKA — This pig never does!

UBU TRUMP — Michel Flynn, thank Czar Putin, for his help I'll build him Trump Hotel Moscow. He can have the Penthouse as long as he keeps inviting me to his orgies.

Scene IV

Trump tower

UBU TRUMP — What do you want, Messenger?

THE MESSENGER — You are summoned, Sir, in the name of the King and the President of the United States of America.

UBU TRUMP — Holly Mecca shit, great balls of fire, by my green dick, I've been found out! They'll chop my head off, Saudi style!

(Pausing)

I'll just say it was Ubu Ivanka and Michael Flynn.

MICHAEL FLYNN — Ah! Shit head. If you do that...

UBU IVANKA — Oh, Papa Ubu! If you succeed in killing him, I'll give you new golf balls, Viagra and 12 Russian hookers!

UBU TRUMP — I'll just kill him.

Scene V
The Palace

UBU TRUMP *(stuttering)*. It wasn't me, you know! It was Ubu Ivanka and Michael Flynn.

THE KING — What is the matter, Ubu Trump?

MICHAEL FLYNN — He's is out of his mind. He had 10 Big Macs.

THE KING — Ubu Trump, I am anxious to reward you for your numerous services as the Captain of dragons. I'll also make you Governor of Texas today.

UBU TRUMP — Dear Majesty, I don't know how to thank you.

THE KING — Don't thank me, Ubu Trump. Just be there tomorrow at the big parade tomorrow.

Scene VI
Trump tower

UBU TRUMP — My good friends, let's finalise our conspiracy.

MICHAEL FLYNN — Speak, Ubu Trump

UBU TRUMP — I want to slip Polonium-210 in the King's lunch, Russian style poisoning. He'll disintegrate briefly like Arafat and most of Putin's foes.

ALL — High five, filthy pig!

UBU TRUMP — Let Michael Flynn share his idea.

MICHAEL FLYNN — I think we should whack him with a sword ISIS style.

ALL — Yes, it is noble and easily done.

UBU TRUMP — Are you aware, by the way, that the King would award me with his postal office building in Washington if I snitch on you?

UBU IVANKA — Oh! Traitor, coward, nasty servile cheapskate!

ALL — Boo, Ubu Trump!

UBU TRUMP — Hey! Gentlemen, calm yourselves. I'll take the risk for you! Michael Flynn, you're in charge of slicing the King in two!

PAUL MANAFORT — Wouldn't it be better to gang up on him at once screaming and yelling? We'd have a better chance of winning over the troops.

UBU TRUMP — Ok, I'll try to step on his feet. He'll jump back, and I'll say: SHIT, and on that signal you will all jump on him and scream.

ALL — Hurrah

Act 2
Scene I
The King's Palace

THE KING — Madam Chelsea, you were very impertinent this morning to Ubu Trump, Knight of my orders and owner of countless Trump Real Estate. Therefore I forbid you to appear at my parade.

THE QUEEN — But who will defend you?

THE KING — Madam, you tire me with this nonsense.

CHELSEA — I submit, my King!

THE QUEEN — Really, my Lord, are you determined to go to this parade?

THE KING — Why not, my Lady?

THE QUEEN — Have I not dreamed of Ubu Trump striking you with his many weapons and throwing you into the river, with the Polish crown and the US flag upon his head?

THE KING — What madness! Ubu Trump is a very fine Gentleman who would let himself be torn apart by wild horses for my service.

THE QUEEN AND CHELSESA — What idiocy!

THE KING — Keep your opinions to yourself, young monkey. And you, my lady, to prove how little I fear Ubu Trump, I'm going to the parade without sword.

THE QUEEN — ...Fatal imprudence!... I won't see you living again.

They leave.

THE QUEEN — Chelsea, come into the Chapel with me, pray for your father and your brothers.

Scene II

The parade ground

THE KING — Noble Ubu Trump, come to inspect the troops.

UBU TRUMP — Coming, Sir, coming.

Ubu's men surround the King.

THE KING — Ah! There is the regiment of Danzig horses. My word, they are very beautiful!

UBU TRUMP — Do you think so? They appear to me to be very miserable. Look at this one. *(To the soldier)* How long has it been since you washed yourself, you worthless clown?

THE KING — But this soldier is very clean. What is the matter with you, Ubu Trump?

UBU TRUMP — This!

He stamps on the King's foot.

THE KING — Wretch!

UBU TRUMP — Shit! To me, my men!

MICHAEL FLYNN — Hurrah! Forward!

All strike the King with swards.

THE KING — Oh! Help! Help! Holy Virgin, I'm gonna die!

MICHAEL FLYNN — That does it! He is dead!

UBU TRUMP — Ah! I have the crown! I captured all his votes. Now for the others.

MICHAEL FLYNN — Death to the entire family!

The King's sons and entourage run away. All pursue them.

Scene III

At the Palace

THE QUEEN — At last I begin to feel reassured.

CHELSEA — You don't have any cause to fear.

An awful clamour is heard outside.

THE QUEEN — What is that dreadful noise?

CHELSEA — Ah! What do I see !? My two brothers pursued by Ubu Trump and his men!

THE QUEEN — Oh my God! Holy Virgin. They're losing ground.

CHELSEA — The whole army is following Ubu Trump. The King is not there. Horror! Help!

THE QUEEN — Boleslas is dead! He received a bullet.

CHELSEA — Hey! *(Ladislas turns around.)* Defend yourself! Hurrah for Ladislas!

THE QUEEN — Oh! He's surrounded.

MICHAEL FLYNN — This is the end of him. Just cut him in two, like a sausage.

THE QUEEN — Alas! These madmen penetrate the Palace. They're coming up the stairs!

The noise increases.

THE QUEEN AND CHELSEA *(on their knees)* — My God, defend us.

CHELSEA — Oh! That Ubu Trump! The wretched rogue!

Scene IV

The Palace. Ubu Trump and his men burst in.

UBU TRUMP — Hey! Chelsea.

CHELSEA — By God, I will defend my mother to the death! The first one to take a step dies!

UBU TRUMP — Oh, Michael Flynn, I'm scared! Let me out of here.

A SOLDIER *(advances)* — Surrender, Chelsea!

CHELSEA — Hold, Hooligan! Here's your punishment!

Chelsea splits open the Soldier's skull.

THE QUEEN — Hold your ground, Chelsea! Hold your ground!

MANY *(advancing)* — Chelsea, we promise to spare your life.

CHELSEA — Scoundrels, scrotums, mercenary monkeys!

She makes a windmill with her sword, and massacres them.

UBU TRUMP — Oh! I'll finish this thing just the same.

CHELSEA — Mother, save yourself by the secret staircase.

THE QUEEN — And you, my daughter, and you?

CHELSEA — I'll follow.

UBU TRUMP — Try and catch the queen! Ah, she's gone!

Scene V

The Palace

UBU TRUMP — No! I won't do it! Do you want to ruin me with this nonsense?!

MICHAEL FLYNN — But in short, Ubu Trump, don't you see that the people are awaiting a happy event?

UBU IVANKA — If you don't have meats and gold distributed, you'll be overthrown within two hours.

UBU TRUMP — Meats, yes! Gold, no! Slaughter three old horses.

That's good enough for such monkeys.

UBU IVANKA — Monkey yourself!

UBU TRUMP — For the last time, I want to become richer. I won't release a single coin.

UBU IVANKA — Ubu Trump, you have in your hands all the treasures of Poland and the USA.

JARED KUSHNER — But Ubu Trump, if you don't make any distributions, the people will not want to pay their taxes.

UBU TRUMP — Is this really true?

UBU IVANKA — Yes! Jared is right. They can call the tea party on you and troll you.

UBU TRUMP — Oh, then I agree to all. Invite millions of people and cook a hundred and fifty cows and sheep.

Scene VI
The Court of the Palace full of people.

PEOPLE — There's the King, the President of the United States! Long live the King-President Ubu Trump! Hurrah!

UBU TRUMP *(throwing gold)* — Catch. This is for you. It hardly amuses me to give you money. At least promise me you'll pay your taxes, stay in my hotels and buy Ivanka's clothing.

ALL — Yes, yes!

MICHAEL FLYNN — Look, how they squabble. What a battle over this gold!

UBU TRUMP — It's truly amazing. There's even someone with his skull cracked open. This is more exciting than Syria.

JARED KUSHNER — Let's repeat this more often.

UBU TRUMP — What a beautiful spectacle! Bring more cases of gold.

JARED KUSHNER — Let's make a race. We can also use Paul Manaford's Ukrainian gold.

UBU TRUMP — *(To the* **people***)* My friends, do you see this cases of gold? It contains three Million Polsky-dollarsky. We'll do a race. Line up.

ALL — Yes! Long live Ubu Trump! What a good King-President! Your ratings will go through the roof!

All the people line up at the far end of the courtyard.

UBU TRUMP — One, two, three! Are you ready?

ALL — Yes! Yes!

UBU TRUMP — Go!

They start running and falling over themselves. Screaming and tumult.

UBU TRUMP — A bloody stampede!

PAUL MANAFORT — They are approaching! They are approaching!

UBU TRUMP — Hey! The first one is losing ground!

UBU IVANKA — No! He is regaining it.

JARED KUSHNER — Oh! He's losing, he's losing!

UBU TRUMP — Oh. Great, it's George Zimmerman who came in first.

ALL — Long live George Zimmerman! Long live George Zimmerman!

Geroge Zimmerman is allowed to enter the Palace.

GEORGE ZIMMERMAN — My King-President, I really don't know how to thank you for helping me win this race without even running. I also still owe you gratitude for acquitting me in the Trayvon Martin case.

UBU TRUMP — Better thank Jeff Sessions, he arranged it. And please, hide your bribe money. ***UBU TRUMP** Addressing the crowd* All you people, come in and dine. My palace doors are open today. Please honour me

PEOPLE — Long live Ubu Trump! He is the best King-President!

An orgy ensues that continues until the following day.

Act 3

Scene I

The Palace

UBU IVANKA — Papa Ubu, all is very well, but we have to economise. You should take money from the poor and hand it to the super-rich like us. Otherwise, we'll lose their support.

UBU TRUMP — By my green dick, ok, let's ride the phynance horse.

UBU IVANKA — But we still owe a great deal to Michael Flynn and need to pay him.

UBU TRUMP — Do me a favour, don't speak of that Buffoon. He can kiss my ass.

UBU IVANKA — You're making a mistake, Papa Ubu. He'll turn against you, join Czar Putin, align with Chelsea.

UBU TRUMP — I am no more concerned about that small man as I am about Chelsea.

UBU IVANKA — Hey? Do you think you're done with Chelsea?

UBU TRUMP — That young monkey?

UBU IVANKA — Papa Ubu, try to win over Chelsea with your kindness.

UBU TRUMP — More money to hand out? Oh! No! You've already made me waste millions.

UBU IVANKA — Watch out Papa Ubu, these two will strangle you with Trump ties.

UBU TRUMP — Well, you will be with me in the grave.

UBU IVANKA — Listen, Chelsea has justice on her side and now you are even alienating your security advisor, with his Russian connection and his fake media empire.

UBU TRUMP — Ah, dirt! Isn't truth as worthy as untruth? Stop harassing me, Ubu Trump.

Ubu Ivanka runs away

Scene II
The Great Hall of the White Palace

UBU TRUMP — Bring in the caskets and the Kalashnikovs! --- Now, bring in the senators! Let's drain the swamp.

The senators are brutally shoved in.

UBU IVANKA — Restrain yourself, Ubu Trump.

UBU TRUMP — I order to enrich the Kingdom, Washington and the Trump Dynasty, I'm going to kill every single one of you senators and take your possessions.

SENATORS —Horror! To us, people, soldiers, voters and the media, Horror!

UBU TRUMP — Bring the first senator and pass me my Kalashnikov. Those condemned to death go to my debraining machine. *(To the 1st Senator)* Who are you, Buffoon?

FIRST SENATOR — Buck, Senator of Alaska.

UBU TRUMP — What's your income?

FIRST SENATOR — 500,000 Polsky-dollarsky a year.

UBU TRUMP — Condemned!

He shoots the Senator and puts him down the hole.

UBU IVANKA — What ferocity!

UBU TRUMP — Second Senator, who are you?

(The Senator says nothing.)

UBU TRUMP — You are going to answer, dirt-bag?

SECOND SENATOR — Posen, Senator of Massachusetts.

UBU TRUMP — Excellent! An east coaster, that's all I want to know. A bullet in the brain, just the way we would do it in black neighbourhoods! Third Senator, who are you? You have a dirty head.

THIRD SENATOR — Roy Moore, Senator of Alabama.

UBU TRUMP — Oh, the pedophile?

THIRD SENATOR — Ubu Trump, have pity, I'm just like you..

UBU TRUMP — Ok, get out of here, but organise a party for us. *(Trump to Michael Flynn whispering)*, After the party, spry some bullets in his head like we did with Philando Castile. – *(loud)* Fourth Senator, who are you?

FOURTH SENATOR — Antony Weiner, Senator of New York.

UBU TRUMP — I love all these child molesters in the senate, what's your income?

FOURTH SENATOR — I'm fucking broke for paying so many settlements.

UBU TRUMP — I shoot you for foul language and for not granting me favourable building permits. Next, who are you?

GOVERNOR — Chris Christy, Governor of New Jersey.

UBU TRUMP — I recognise you. You should have closed the bridge in both directions forever and flooded the tunnels to keep your junkies and opioid addicts out of New York City. What kind of shit are you sniffing? OK, I will strangle you to death like Eric Garner for selling loosies!

UBU IVANKA — You are too ferocious, Ubu Trump.

UBU TRUMP — Hey! I'm becoming richer. New Jersey, Texas and Massachusetts are rich states and they enter exclusively into my personal portfolio. I'm going to litter these states with Trump properties, Casinos, and Trump factories filled with illegals. -- Senator Herald. I know you, Remind me of your state?

SENATOR HERALD — California.

UBU TRUMP — You only won California because of the Mexican voter fraud. Bullets in your head. But don't dare to run away unarmed like Walter Scott. --- Let's go fast. I have to go tweet. All senators in the mobile van. Drive them to death.

The Senators are driven to death in multiple vans.

UBU TRUMP — Hurray, I drained the swamp. Now, let's make new laws. I make putrid laws.

SEVERAL ELECTED OFFICIALS — This we've got to see.

UBU TRUMP — First I'm going to first reform justice: I need only one supreme judge and that is me. Clarence Thomas can stay and organise a new department for the propagation of misogyny and sexual assault. Now, let's proceed the executive branch of government and budgeting.

SEVERAL ELECTED OFFICIALS — We oppose all change.

UBU TRUMP — Shut up! From now on, all elected officials will no longer be paid.

ALL ELECTED OFFICIALS — And what will we live on? We are poor.

UBU TRUMP — You can pocket all fines you impose and keep all possessions of those you sentence to death.

FIRST SECRETARY OF STATE — Horror!

SECOND — Infamy!

THIRD — Scandal!

FOURTH — Indignity!

UBU IVANKA — Hey, what are you doing, Papa Ubu Trump? Who's to render justice now?

UBU TRUMP — Me! You will see how well things will go.

ALL — We refuse to work under those circumstances.

UBU TRUMP — Shut up, you brainless tarts. Otherwise, I'll have you debrained like the special Counsel Robert Mueller ! --- And now, gentlemen, we proceed to the matters of taxes.

FINANCIERS — There's nothing that needs change.

UBU TRUMP — But I want everything changed! I want to keep half of the taxes for myself.

FINANCIERS — How excessive and unlawful.

UBU TRUMP — Gentlemen, we'll quadruple the taxes on property, double those on trade and industry, and put new taxes on those who marry.

FIRST FINANCIER — But that's unrealistic, Ubu Trump.

SECOND FINANCIER — It's absurd and unlawful.

UBU TRUMP — You dare argue with me, you shit phynanciers! Let's decapitate them for a change.

They stuff the financiers in the hole and cut off their heads.

UBU IVANKA — But really. Papa Ubu, what kind of a King-President are you? You slaughter everybody.

UBU TRUMP — No worries, my daughter, I keep the most loyal like you and your husband Jared.

UBU IVANKA — No more justice? No more phynance?

UBU TRUMP — Wrong, it's now Trump-Justice and Trump-Phynance, my sweet child. I'll go from city to city, from state to state and collect the taxes in person.

Scene III
House of Peasant

A PEASANT (coming in) — Did you hear the big news? King Wenceslas is dead, all nobles had been killed, and young Chelsea ran away to the mountains. Most senators were cold-bloodedly assassinated the same way blacks are shot by police. Funeral homes spill over with debrained bodies. Ubu Trump has seized the throne and stolen all US votes with the help of Czar Putin, WikiLeaks and James Comey.

ANOTHER PEASANT — I come from Krakow-Chicago where I saw them carry away the bodies of more than 300 congressmen. They also killed 500 local and state officials, and it appears that they are going to collect taxes twice. Ubu Trump even does it even himself.

ALL — God! What will become of us?

PEASANT — Ubu Trump is awful and his family abominable. He hates Harlem in particular and tweeted how he wants to flood morgues with bodies.

ANOTHER PEASANT — He also introduced a new legal tender, we have now Trump dollars at an exchange rate 10 to 1.

ALL — Decrepit bastard, we're gonna starve to death.

A knock at the door.

PEASANT — Listen! Is that not someone knocking at the door?

THE VOICE OF UBU TRUMP *(outside)* — Horn-belly! Open! Gimme your taxes! We take credit cards, stocks, bonds and Trump-dollars!

The door is demolished. Ubu Trump enters followed by his legion of money-snatchers.

Scene IV

House of Peasant

UBU TRUMP — Which one of you is the oldest? *(A peasant citizen advances.)* What's your name?

IBRAHIM MUSTAFA — Ibrahim Mustafa.

UBU TRUMP — Well then, horn-belly, listen to me, otherwise I cut off your head.

IBRAHIM MUSTAFA — Your Excellency has yet to say anything.

UBU TRUMP — Produce your money immediately. Also, your Polsky-dollarsky debt will stay at the Trump dollar exchange rate.

IBRAHIM MUSTAFA — My lord, we were only supposed to be taxed 152 Polsky-dollarskis and now you are asking for 152 Trump Dollars, which is 10 times more. We paid our taxes already six weeks ago.

UBU TRUMP — It is very possible but I've changed the government. Now, you have to pay all existing taxes twice and the second time in Trump dollars. Only Trump dollars and double taxation will guarantee me a fortune quickly. Don't worry, we will debrain everybody anyway, so what does it matter. Give me all your money.

PEASANTS — Terrible, unfair!

UBU TRUMP — Mustafa, you also didn't obey my Muslim ban, therefore pay my taxes four times albeit that your grand father served already in WWII.

PEASANTS — Ubu Trump! Have mercy on us. We are poor people.

UBU TRUMP — I don't give a shit. Pay or perish.

PEASANTS — We are not able to. We have already paid.

UBU TRUMP — Pay! Or I'll break you with torture! Horn-belly.

ALL — Enough, Revolt! To arms! Long live Chelsea, by God's grace the future Queen and president of Poland and the USA!

UBU TRUMP *(to his tax collectors)* — Kill them all and take everything. You can keep 10 %.

A fight ensues. The house is destroyed, and Mustafa and all others who make it run away. Ubu Trump remains to collect all money and valuables.

Scene V
On a black site, a Secret CIA detention facility

UBU TRUMP — Michael Flynn, you dare to ask me for something. You did a great job killing the king, stealing the Democrats' emails, colluding with Putin, organising Russian money for my business and more. But why did you snitch on me.

MICHAEL FLYNN — Ubu Trump, in the 15 days you've been King-President you've committed more murders than people died in all wars in the middle east. This blood cries for vengeance.

(he turns away and runs)

UBU TRUMP — Hey! My friend, watch your mouth. Don't run away.

Scene VI

The palace at Moscow

CZAR PUTIN — *(Putin read by Yvanka reader)* Was it not you, infamous adventurer, who conspired in the death of my cousin Wenceslas?

MICHAEL FLYNN — My lord, forgive me. I was forced by Ubu Trump.

CZAR PUTIN — That awful liar and imbecile! Anyway, what do you want?

MICHAEL FLYNN — Ubu Trump trumped up conspiracy and collusion charges against me. I barely escaped with my life, riding on horseback for five days and five nights across the steppes to come and implore your gracious mercy.

CZAR PUTIN — What did you bring me as a token of your submission?

MICHAEL FLYNN — King Wenceslas' sword and a detailed plan of all Black Sites, the secret CIA jails. I also got tapes with Ubu Trump contracting syphilis with prostitutes in Moscow.

CZAR PUTIN — I'll take the sword. Please, burn the plans of the Black Sites because it is us building them and maintaining them for the USA. Also, I don't want to owe my victory to treason.

MICHAEL FLYNN — One of the daughters of the former King, young Chelsea, is still alive. We should do everything we can do to restore her to the throne.

CZAR PUTIN — What rank did you hold in the Polish army anyway?

MICHAEL FLYNN — I commanded the 5th regiment of dragoons at Wilna. I was also promised Puerto Rico when I was not yet destroyed by a Hurricane and a US state.

CZAR PUTIN — Good. I name you Sub-Lieutenant in the 10th Cossack regiment, and beware if you turn traitor! If you fight well, you will be rewarded.

MICHAEL FLYNN — I do not lack courage, my Czar.

He goes.

Scene VII

At Trump tower

UBU TRUMP — Gentlemen, the meeting is now open. First we're going to examine our phynances, then we'll talk about a little system I've invented to control the weather. Also, the Trump-dollar conversion has been a tremendous success.

A COUNCILLOR — Oh, very good indeed, Mister Ubu Trump. We are enchanted by your portraits on each side of the coin.

UBU IVANKA — My image is on the back side, not his. But what a silly man, Ubu Trump is!

UBU TRUMP — Lady of my shit, watch your tongue. Well then, gentlemen, I have informed you that the phynances are going fairly well. On all sides one sees only burning houses, and people bending under the weight of our taxes. What an entertaining chaos.

UBU IVANKA — Also, we are forcing people to wear my clothing line.

UBU TRUMP — We have now obligatory Trump-care with 100% co-payments

A COUNCILLOR — Yes, that works very well with kickbacks from insurance companies and hospitals on top of it.

UBU TRUMP — A tremendous success. And are my new taxes working?

UBU IVANKA — Unfortunately, not. The tax on marriage has produced only 110 Trump-dollars.

A messenger is dropping off a letter.

UBU TRUMP — Ah! He left this letter, buffoonette, I'm afraid. It must be from Michael Flynn.

UBU IVANKA — Precisely. Czar Putin welcomed him very well, he's going to invade our lands to re-establish Chelsea. He swears you will be killed.

UBU TRUMP — I am afraid! I think I'm dying. Oh, poor man that I am. All saints, protect me! I will give you money.

He weeps and sobs.

UBU IVANKA — There's only one way out, Papa Ubu.

UBU TRUMP — Which is what, my love?

UBU IVANKA — War!

ALL — War, Praise God! War, Praise the Tea Party! War is noble! War it is, use your nukes!

UBU TRUMP — Yes, since we have nukes we should use them! *(Pausing)* But do you have an idea how much an army costs? Airplanes, rockets, bombs, and nuclear arms cost even more so. The Trump family business is not yet invested in the military industrial complex. So far we've made money only with hospitality services. War is expensive. I already hated to send a single soldier to rescue people in Puerto Rico. By the way, I want hurricane Maria be renamed Hurricane Trump. For that naming problem my weather controlling power wasn't able to reroute the storm to Mexico.

COUNCILLOR — Ubu Trump, there is no choice. Let's organise the army and invade Mexico on our way home.

UBU TRUMP — I'll pay for the war, but only if we win!

COUNCILLOR — We need to centralise all finances for war.

UBU TRUMP — No, no! I'm going to kill you. I don't want to spend money. You collect all money you can get from the poor.

ALL — Long live war!

Scene VIII

The encampment before Warsaw Washington.

SOLDIERS — Long live Poland and the USA! Long live Ubu Trump and all his brand names!

UBU TRUMP — Hey, Ubu Ivanka, give me my breastplate, my swagger and my AK47. But I need somebody to carry all this it for me.

UBU IVANKA — Listen to this coward!

UBU TRUMP — Remember, the Russians advance and they're out to kill me and you.

UBU IVANKA — You're looking like an armed pumpkin.

UBU TRUMP — Bring me also the Horse of Phynance.

UBU IVANKA — Your horse won't be able to carry you. It hasn't eaten anything for five days and is nearly dead.

UBU TRUMP — Possibly, but they wanted me to pay 12 coins a day for this horse.

(Ubu Ivanka blushes, and lowers her eyes.)

All right, bring me another beast, but I won't go on foot. Horn-belly!

Henchman Lap leads in an enormous horse.

UBU IVANKA — He is indeed an imbecile. He can't even climb a horse by himself.

UBU TRUMP — Fizzihorn, I'm off to war and I will kill everybody.

UBU IVANKA — Good luck, Papa Ubu! Kill Czar Putin and Chelsea.

UBU TRUMP — For sure twisting off their noses and teeth, extracting their tongues and water boarding.

The army moves off to the sound of fanfares.

Act 4

Scene I

The town square in Warsaw-Washington.

CHELSEA — Forward, my friends! Long live the King of Poland, President Washington and the USA! That old rogue Ubu Trump will soon be gone. We also will get the old witch, Ubu Ivanka, and all the other bastards. I will lead the march to re-establish the dynasty of my family.

ALL — Long live Chelsea!

CHELSEA — I'll revoke all Ubu Trump taxes and get rid of the Ubu Trump dollars.

ALL — Hurrah! Forward! Let's run to the palace and slaughter the whole brood.

The crowd launches stones.

FIRST GUARD — All the windows are broken.

Ubu Ivanka runs away pursued by all the Poles. Shots and hail of stones.

Scene II

The Polish army on the march in the Ukraine-Pennsylvania

UBU TRUMP — Ham of God! Head of a cow! We are going to perish because we die of thirst and tiredness. Soldier, have the kindness to carry my phynance box, and you, Scaramucci, take charge of the shit-chisel and physics-stick to relieve us, because, I repeat, we are tired.

The soldiers obey.

JARRED KUSHNER — It is astonishing that the Russians don't appear.

UBU TRUMP — Well, it is regrettable that the state of our phynances doesn't permit us to have an army of self-driving cars and self-fighting robots.

JARRED KUSHNER — See, there's Steve Bannon appearing in a hurry.

UBU TRUMP — What's bothering him, this boy?

STEVE BANNON — All is lost. The Poles are revolting. Ubu Ivanka has fled to the mountains.

UBU TRUMP — Bird of night, beast of misfortune, owl in leg warmers! Where do you finish with this nonsense? It's just one thing after another. And who did it? Chelsea, I bet.

STEVE BANNON — Yes, noble Ubu Trump, in Warsaw Washington she rules..

UBU TRUMP — Bannon, Boy of my shit, if I believed you I'd make the whole army go back the same way it came. But, the Russians are not far off, Czar Putin wants all our databases, phynances and physics. He already snatched Edward Snowden away from us.

GENERAL MAD DOG — Ubu Trump, don't you see the Russians coming?

UBU TRUMP — It is true! The Russians! And now I am screwed! We are on a hill and exposed on all sides. Are there any way for me to get away? I'm scared, I suffer from diarrhoea. You must fight and protect me.

THE ARMY — The Russians! The enemy!

UBU TRUMP — You go, you go, Boutez en avant! Take up your positions. I stay on this hill and you go down and fight. Circle around me down there. Put in your rifles as many bullets as possible. A bullet must equal a dead Russian. I will stay inside the windmill and will fire with my phynance-gun through the window though I hate to be poor again. – General Mad Dog! When will they attack and what's the time now.

GENERAL MAD DOG — 11 in the morning.

UBU TRUMP — Then we shall eat lunch because these lazy Russians won't attack before noon. Esteemed Mad Dog, get everybody ready and begin the Song of war phynances. Sing: starvation for them, fine dining for us.

Mad Dog leaves.

SOLDIERS — Long live Ubu Trump!

UBU TRUMP — Oh, all these brave people. I adore them!

A Russian cannonball arrives

UBU TRUMP — Ah! I'm scared. God, I'm dead! And yet, no – I've no injuries.

Scene IV
Battle field
A CAPTAIN — Ubu Trump, the Russians attack started ahead of time.

UBU TRUMP — What do you expect me to do about it? It wasn't me who told them to. They usually don't do shit before noon. Gentlemen of Phynances, let us fight. Let's spread fake news, bribery and attack the media.

A second cannonball — Ubu Trump is bowled over, the cannonball bouncing up and down on his belly

GENERAL MAD DOG — A second cannonball! I'm getting out of here. Not a good time for lunch.

He flees.

UBU TRUMP — Ah, I've had enough. It rains lead and iron here and it could damage my precious skin and my china. You should all descend into the war theatre.

All descend quickly. The battle erupts. They disappear into torrents of smoke at the foot of the hill.

RUSSIAN SOLDIERS — For God and Czar Putin!

STEVE BANNON — Ah! I'm dead!

UBU TRUMP — Good, I couldn't take you anymore. I think I have to soon become a democrat again.

A RUSSIAN — Ubu Trump, I'll shoot you.

He shoots him with a revolver.

UBU TRUMP — Oh no! I am wounded! I'm done for! I'm buried! Except that he missed! Ah! I got him! *(He rips him open.)* Now, we start winning! Report to Fox News, we're winning!

GENERAL MAD DOG — Forward! Let's press home our advantage! Victory is ours!

UBU TRUMP — You think so? So far I feel on my forehead more bumps than laurels.

RUSSIAN CAVALRY —Hurrah! Make way for Czar Putin!

The Czar Putin enters, accompanied by Michael Flynn, disguised.

A POLE —Ah! Lord! Save what you can! There's Czar Putin!

ANOTHER — Oh, my God! He's crossing the moat.

A THIRD — Biff! Boff! There's four of them stunned by that big bastard of a lieutenant.

MICHAEL FLYNN — Ah! I had enough.

UBU TRUMP — Forward, my friends! Catch this blighter! We'll make mincemeat of these Muscovites! Victory is ours!

ALL — Forward! Hurrah! Ham of God! Get the big feller!

MICHAEL FLYNN — I have fallen.

UBU TRUMP *(recognising him)* — Ah, it is you, Flynn! Ah, my friend, we are happy to see you die. I'm going to cook you slowly! Gentlemen of Phynances, light a fire.

Something hits Ubu Trump

Ah! No! Ah! I'm dead. It is at least a cannonball I received. Ah! my God, forgive me my sins. Yes, it is definitely a cannonball. Now, I believe in God as well. Rescue me!

GENERAL MAD DOG — You've been only shot with a cap-pistol, not a cannon ball. Your only slightly hurt in your butt.

UBU TRUMP — Ah! How encouraging. You get a raise, Mad Dog.

GENERAL MAD DOG — Ubu Trump, we advance on all fronts.

UBU TRUMP — Oh! my bollocks!

GENERAL MAD DOG — Don't sit, go take the Czar Putin instead.

UBU TRUMP — You do it for me! Take this shit-sword, do your duty, and you, money-crook, don't remain behind. Physics-stick, emulate them. Slaughter, abuse and torture the Muscovites and their Czar. Forward, my Horse of Phynance must survive!

General Mad Dog charges at the Czar.
A RUSSIAN OFFICER — Watch out, Your Majesty!
The Czar evades a shot and pursues Ubu Trump.

UBU TRUMP — Holy Virgin, this fanatic pursues me! I've got to escape, great God!

He jumps the moat. The Czar falls in.

CZAR PUTIN — Bollocks! I've fallen in.

POLES — Hurrah! Czar Putin is down!

UBU TRUMP — I hardly dare turn around!. My physics-stick and bravery worked marvels. There's no doubt that I would have completely killed him if an inexplicable terror had not come upon me and annulled in us the effects of our courage. But we had to suddenly turn around, and owe our preservation only to the solidity of our Horse of Phynances.

The Russian dragoons charge their Kalashinkows, and rescue the Czar Putin.

UBU TRUMP — Ah! We were so close to finish the bastard off. But now, that's our cue to get out of here. Backward!

POLES — Every man for himself!

UBU TRUMP — Let's go! What mess.! How am I going to get out of this mess? *(He is attacked and knocked over by Russians.)* Hey you! Don't kill me!, Wait! Taste the wrath of Mister Phynance. I write you a check. You can cash right away.

Ubu Trump writes some checks bribing the Russians who attack him. Now they are gone. Let's save ourselves – and quick! – while Mad Dog isn't looking.

He runs off, then we see the Czar Putin and the Russian army pursuing the Poles.

Scene V

A cave in Lithuania, Pennsylvania. It snows.

UBU TRUMP — Ah! What a wretched time. It's freezing enough to split a rock and my horse of Phynance is badly hurt.

SCARAMUCCI — Hey! Ubu Trump, are you done with your terror and your flight?

UBU TRUMP — Yes. I'm not afraid any more, but I must flee again.

PREIBUS *(aside)* — What a swine!

UBU TRUMP — Hey, Preibus, How does it go?

PREIBUS — Sir, As well as it can and it could be worse. I can't extract the bullet.

UBU TRUMP — That's good. You were always wanting to strike others. Me, I displayed the greatest courage and slaughtered four enemies by my own hands, not counting those that had already died.

PREIBUS — Do you know, what became of little boy Bannon?

SCARAMUCCI — He received a friendly bullet in the head.

UBU TRUMP — I regret it, but it was mine by mistake.

PREIBUS — The Trump presidency is over.

UBU TRUMP — You wish. You horny bastard.

SCARAMUCCI — I'm dying of hunger.

UBU TRUMP — I'm hungry, me! But I see Russians everywhere. My God! Oh!

Ubu Trump falls asleep.

PREIBUS — I wish I knew if what Bannon said is true, whether Ubu Ivanka is indeed dethroned. It's not impossible.

SCARAMUCCI — You're right. So it's now really time to abandon Ubu Trump. He is useless, he will never really deliver white supremacism!

Scene VII
Harlem morgue
Ubu Trump speaking while delirious on his deathbed.

Czar Putin, don't cut, don't cut me into pieces, I'm already dead, I was shoot by Michael Flynn who is now fucking Chelsea. This deplorable traitor, rapist. Czar Putin, you plagiarised my precious script and defeated my horse of Phynance! You are so sad! And I'm dead, I can't breath; I can't breath. I swallowed all my gold, but blue lives matter. Now, I'm wretched, I'm wretched off the earth! Czar Putin, we are too close to the sharp Muslim moon, to improvised explosive devises. I've been dead a long time. It's Chelsea who killed me. I am buried at Arlington cathedral, next to presidents and King Wenscelav. Next to my native sons I hated so much. Czar Putin, let me confess: I loved when you fucked my ass blue in Moscow and recently in Hamburg. I call this truly an anal collusion. I adore colliding with you, Vladimir. Also know, I'm truly a Fox News sent beast of Satan willing to slaughter people of colour! I'm an O'Reilley solider and took all people's money, minds, education, healthcare and health. I dope them to death! I used fentanyl myself as my lubrication through the election hell, to get a ride on the pope mobile, on air force one to heaven, protected from cabbage throwers and pink pussy-parade lovers who yell urbi et orbi for climate change. Shit fake newsers. By my green dick: Welcome, to a gentrified death in a Harlem morgue. Czar Putin, you're fired. From now on your Trump-Putin. We both grabbed the pussy of the Russian Queen. My lease is expired. I'm fired, Trumpputin. What a shithole country, my country …

Ubu Trump falls silent and dies.

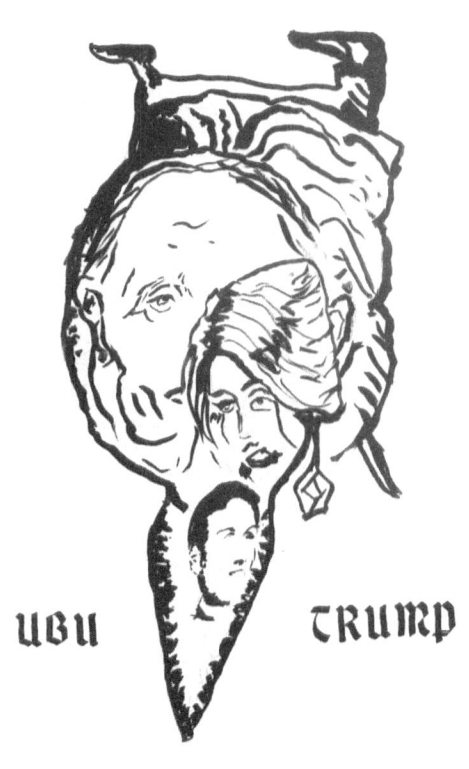

Trump tower

UBU TRUMP: Shit!

UBU IVANKA: Oh! such language! Papa Ubu Trump, what a pig you are!

UBU TRUMP: Watch out I'll kill you!

UBU IVANKA: It's not me, you ought to kill, it's someone else

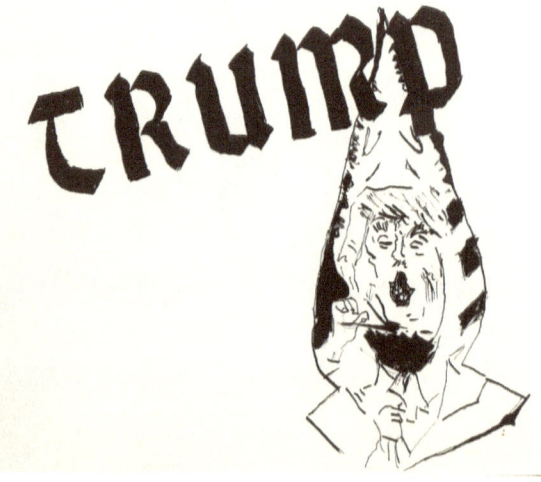

Year One: Our President Ubu
Charles Simic

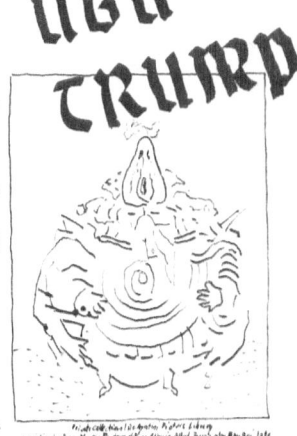

The only character I can think of in world literature who resembles Donald Trump is Pere Ubu in the play *Ubu Roi* ("Ubu the King") by Alfred Jarry that famously opened and closed in Paris on December 10, 1896, after starting a riot. A parody of Shakespeare's *Macbeth* and now a classic of the theatre of the absurd and the forerunner of the Dada and Surrealism movements, the play is a depiction of the lust for power, full of insolent nonsense and violent horseplay. Pere Ubu is a buffoonish pretender to the throne of Poland, a brutal and greedy megalomaniac who, after killing off the royal family, starts murdering his own population in order to rob them of their money. One audience member at the premiere of the play, the Irish poet William Butler Yeats, was aghast at what he had witnessed and reputedly said afterward: "What more is possible? After us, the Savage God."

Recently going over some pieces I've written for the Daily since 2013, on the Republican primaries and debates, and the presidential election, I remember thinking of Ubu while watching Trump back then. Even in the company of such awful human beings as Ben Carson, Ted Cruz, and Carly Fiorina, Trump stood out with his boorishness and malevolence — as when he announced to rapturous cheers of the audience that he would bring back waterboarding and make it a "hell of a lot worse," or called out to his followers to beat up a heckler at one of his rallies where those of our fellow citizens who miss the days of public lynchings came to hear their champion. I hate everyone you hate, was his message over and over again, and these numbskulls who can't even tell the differences between an honest man and a crook nudged each other, knowing exactly whom he had in

Jarry's silly play that so shocked his contemporaries doesn't come close to the antics we read about and see every day. At this rate, in the not-too-distant future, we may all be, in effect, lobotomized by our exposure to Trump's presidency and not even twitch when we come across such breaking news items as these:

President Trump has ordered a naval blockade of Switzerland.

Wayne LaPierre was appointed to the Supreme Court to replace Justice Ginsberg. Asked if he plans to quit as head of the NRA, he glared at the reporters and walked out of the press conference carrying an assault rifle over his shoulder.

Space Aliens' Bible Found in the Nevada desert. They worship President Trump and First Lady Melania.

Jihad is over in the Middle East. The president has struck a deal with their leaders to have their followers enroll in some of the many Trump Universities that have sprung up all over the region and learn how to sell real estate in the desert.

UBU TRUMP,

or

How 19th-century French literature predicted Donald Trump's retro-autocratic futurism

LINDA NORDEN — Tell me a little bit about Alfred Jarry's Ubu. Why did you chose to rewrite him?

RAINER GANAHL — Alfred Jarry was a tragi-comic modernist figure, the quintessential poet-artist who was also a self-destructive loser and died at just 34 in 1907. Yet he managed to influence literature and art for a century to come. Jarry did not really leave any oeuvre, but a bunch of writings, text fragments, plays and graphic works that were all embedded in a drug and alcohol-driven universe of crazy anecdotes, love stories, including with Oscar Wilde, and personal recklessness. His Ubu Roi (King Ubu) was not even written by him alone, but co-written with two high school friends who thought of it as a literary diatribe against an annoying teacher. Jarry ran with it from his native little French town and made it into a literary scandal in Paris. He kept changing it and changing it and produced numerous versions. Jarry clearly stylized himself as an Ubu-esque character, took on weird linguistic and behavioral mannerisms and didn't refrain even from threatening and shooting at his critics with a pistol he carried with him called "bulldog." King Ubu, Papa Ubu, Ubu Cocu (Ubu Cuckolded), Ubu Enchaîné (Ubu in Chains) and other versions produced by Jarry symbolized a narcissistically damaged, insecure dictator who accumulated as much power as he could by any means and terrorized everybody. This all happened just before the WWI, which was essentially a colonialist war. During that war, in Zurich, Jarry's Ubu Roi was presented at Cabaret Voltaire, which inspired me to revist this piece for my Dada Lenin project, since it can be assumed that Lenin himself – who lived opposite the Cabaret at Spiegelgasse – attended the performance. So after having already rewritten this theater play for a Ubu Lenin, it became quickly clear that I also must rewrite it as Ubu Trump, since this president resembles Ubu King in many many ways: vulgar, loud, insecure, narcissistic, brutal, and with disastrous judgment that will bring defeat upon his people and himself.

LN — Why stage the Ubu Lenin play in a funeral home in Harlem?

RG — This play is independent of any particular presentation or site. It could be read or presented between friends at a dinner table, in bed with a lover or at a theater.

But given the fact that I've been living in central Harlem for more than two decades, and that I'm surrounded by morgues and churches, I started to take this option of presentation into account. I also enjoy finding locations myself. Thanks to my notary public, who runs an actual funeral home, I started to become more curious and familiar with these somehow scary, taboo places. We do not want to have anything to do with a morgue since that represents the last transitory stop on our journeys and when we enter it's usually for a sad, tragic last moment.

I realized this funeral home could not only house a public that is mourning a private loss, but also a frustrated public that's suffering a collective political loss. Better than churches, funeral parlors do not relate to any religious belief system. Ubu Trump as a play is very bloody with themes of murder, torture and war that build on a core struggle for power.

LN — I feel like there's a large part of the community you're re-purposing—your "enterprising" use of the funeral home—might offend. People who believe in the sanctity of death. But I was very taken by this performance in that space. I'm often suspicious when a spontaneous, inspired idea becomes fetishized or over-extended. But one of the things I like best in your work is the way you find such inspired sites for each project, as something takes form in response to the very specific circumstances you respond to so keenly in your day-to-day life. Your sites always feel integrally bound up in the issues and questions they assert, because you look at the neighborhoods and communities you live in so topologically.

I like thinking of your Ubu Trump project as having something to do with the way war takes form.

RG — I owe the entire structure to Alfred Jarry's original Ubu King, which brilliantly anticipated the series of dictators we had to endure during the 20th century, when war was omnipresent. It is stunning how this current president has representatives tell troops in the field that war is imminent while he simultaneously shrinks his diplomatic core down to almost nothing. After all, diplomacy's function is to use means other than war.

LN — How did you decide on characters, besides Trump. And did you know where you wanted play to end before you began?

RG — There is a given textual structure that I respected and did not change the positioning of certain material, which itself seems to have elements lifted from Shakespeare and others. The main characters in Jarry's version are King Ubu; his scheming wife, mostly referred to as Mama Ubu; and King Wenceslas on the other side. Therefore, Ubu Trump is repopulated with Ubu Trump, Ubu Ivanka, the King and Queen Wenceslas and their daughter Chelea. We also have Putin, Jared Kushner, Michael Flynn, and other figures from the current administration. I also give prominence to contemporary sexual predators such as Anthony Weiner and Roy Moore.

LN — Were you modeling your text closely or broadly on Jarry or did you do a lot of the writing yourself.

RG — Many of the newly replaced and introduced protagonists come with lines I modified and adapted for the scenes. It is remarkable how the current president and his advisers are jamming the media stream with vulgarities and falsehoods. We are currently witnessing how public discourse that was once mediated by mainstream news sources has been replaced by social media and fake news sites. Therefore it's not very difficult to scan for material worthy of Ubu. Jarry's premonitory brilliance becomes more and more apparent through these boundless autocratic, proto-fascist, self-propagating revolutionaries and their rampaging disregard for the world. Make America Ubu Again. Somehow I had the feeling that I didn't write anything at all, but merely updated it, resynchronized it with our current presidential tropes and tuned it to our attention economy of followers, sharers and likers.

LN — I'd really love to hear what you were after in each of the characters you shaped for Ubu Trump. Would be great to hear how a certain comment or speech conveyed your sense of behavior and character.

RG — Ubu Trump is here really a combination of Jarry's madman Ubu King and Donald Trump's publicly displayed idiosyncrasies, which my particular exaggerations and usage render slightly more farcical. I wanted to really decontextualize our president's shameless, partisan, and self-serving political actionism by placing into literary-political satire. After all, reading the New York Times on Trump's spontaneous, chaotic decision making and sloganeering already reads like Jarry. And sometimes the reality of our political time seems more authentically captured by comedians than by theory.

LN — I was struck on the night of the Ubu Trump performance by the difference between the performance of the play, which felt more like a declaration, or demonstration, than a question, and by the terrifically curated gathering of art, by so many of your friends and peers, in your home, which you seemed to share as if asking "How about this?" In both cases, you seemed genuinely surprised by the size of the audience or attending group, as if these were both projects you did for yourself. But I'm genuinely curious: who do you think you do the work you do for?

RG — I fully agree with you. Repurposing sensitive spaces can be highly problematic and easily go wrong. I try to be very sensitive and was choosing this site also because of its precarious and meaningful role in society. In Austria, where I grew up, they keep death out of view and when I first saw an actual friend on her final open display in Brooklyn, after a suicide, I was traumatized—even more so since I had never seen a dead person before. Now, death in Harlem is pervasive, given the explosive mix of racism, the high concentration of poor people in sometimes substandard living conditions, police bias, and more. But that already makes us enter the very essence of Ubu Trump, a play where horrific governance creates misery and war.

I think in both cases—my friends' artworks in my house and this performance—I do it for myself as part of a public and imagined community. Some of my circle of friends and imagined friends are not even alive, and I might have missed them by a decade or a century or a continent. I count myself as part of my own community and I sometimes project myself onto others who are there or who I wish would be there.

LN — Are there any more Ubu Trump presentations planned?

RG — Yes. A similar version will be staged in Berlin in January 2018 and another one in Mexico City in April. That one will appear exactly 50 years after the famously problematic Mexican Olympic games of 1968, which resulted in the deaths of hundreds of street protesters. Mexicans, Trump's wall and the ghost of the student massacre will all be making guest appearances in that iteration of Ubu Trump. I am also working on yet another version to present in London, where curator Saim Demican and I will reorient ourselves with Werner Fassbinder's version of Ubu Roi, which he presented at the Anti-Theater in August of 1968

December 2017

Hal Foster: Père Ubu is President!

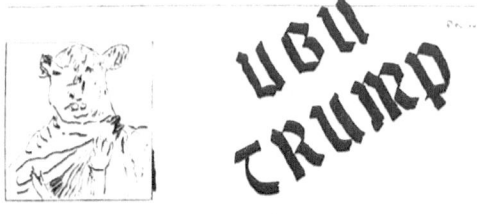

Text by Hal Foster

Sure, "post-truth" is a big problem, but what about "post-shame"? How to challenge a politician who cannot be embarrassed? Or to protest a leader who thrives on the absurd? How to out-dada a dada president? Maybe, when they go very low, we should go even lower, and aim to outrage the outrageous...

Thoughts about a post-shame condition lead to stories about a pre-shame time. The brothers."¹ He brings back the primal father several years later in *Group Psychology and the Analysis of the Ego* (1921), and if *Totem and Taboo* reflects indirectly on democracy, *Group Psychology* does the same with fascism—that is, with the return, long after the democratic decapitation of the king, of the dictatorial ego: not in fact for Freud the mass politics of the time induces a regression to "the group psychology of the horde." "What is thus awakened," he writes, "is the idea of a paramount and dangerous personality towards whom only a passive-masochistic attitude is possible." "The leader of the group," Freud concludes, "is still the dreaded primal father; the group still wishes to be governed by unrestricted force; it has an extreme passion for authority..."²

UBU TRUMP

Shut up
you dirty old shit

UBU IVANKA You are so stupid
UBU TRUMP By my green dick

PUTIN

Merde
TrUMPUTIN

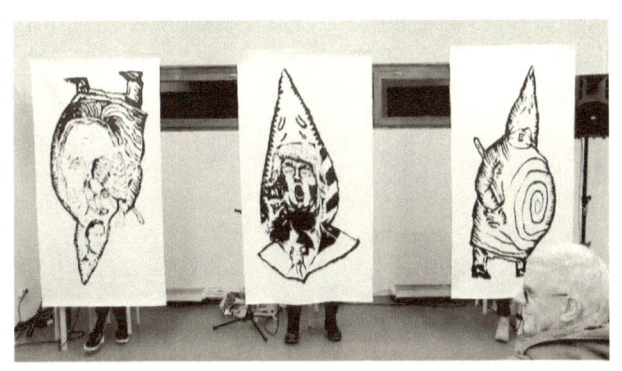

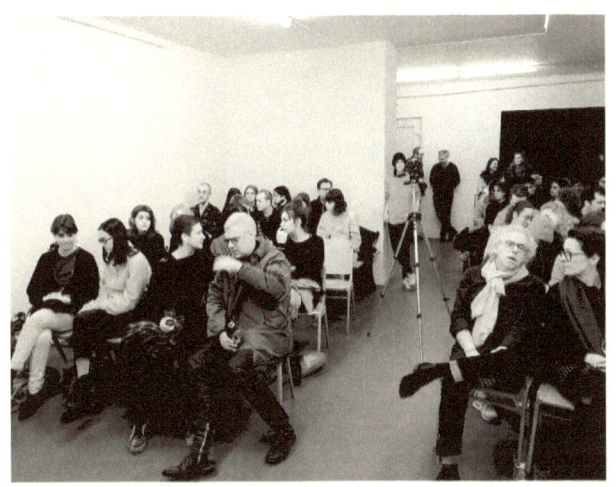

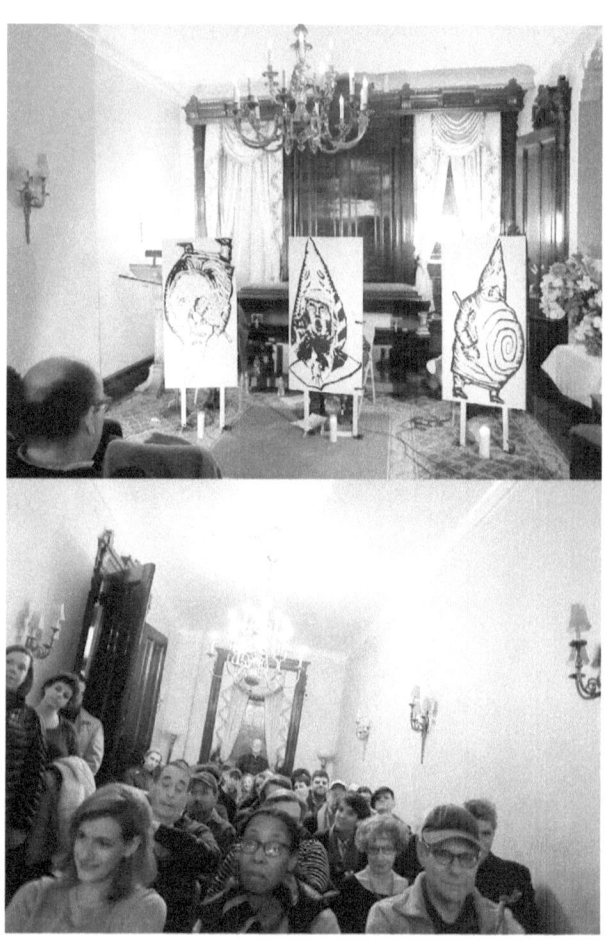

Harlem morgue version
STARRING
Whitney Alexander
Nickolas Calabrese
Rainer Ganahl

December 2017
Daniel Wilhelmina Funeral Home in collaboration with White Columns
110 West 131st Street, New York City

Berlin version
STARRING
Tom Harrison
Lanna Leite
Rainer Ganahl

January 2018
Spike Magazine Berlin in collaboration with Stadium Berlin

by Rainer Ganahl (ganahl.info)
design by Florian Model (florianmodel.com)
Edited by Rachel Corbett

Published by
Kai Matsumiya
kaimatsumiya.com

Copyright Rainer Ganahl 2018

www.ingramcontent.com/pod-product-compliance
Lightning Source LLC
Chambersburg PA
CBHW030517220526
45464CB00006B/2829